DEMARCATIONS

DEMARCATIONS

Jean Follain

Translated and with an Introduction by
Kurt Heinzelman

Host Publications
Austin, TX

Host Publications, Inc. 277 Broadway, Suite 210, New York, NY 10007

Layout and Design	Joe Bratcher and Anand Ramaswamy
Cover Photo	Małgorzata Maj
Jacket Design	Anand Ramaswamy

First Edition

Library of Congress Cataloging-in-Publication Data

Follain, Jean, 1903-1971.
[Territoires. English & French.]
Demarcations / Jean Follain ; translated and with an introduction by Kurt Heinzelman. -- 1st ed.
    p. cm.
ISBN-13: 978-0-924047-87-9 (hardcover : alk. paper)
ISBN-10: 0-924047-87-9 (hardcover : alk. paper)
ISBN-13: 978-0-924047-88-6 (pbk. : alk. paper)
ISBN-10: 0-924047-88-7 (pbk. : alk. paper)
1. Follain, Jean, 1903-1971--Translations into English. I. Heinzelman, Kurt. II. Title.
PQ2611.O612T413 2011
841'.912--dc23
                    2011030037

TABLE OF CONTENTS

AN EXEMPLARY HISTORY OF A MINOR POET:
JEAN FOLLAIN

One of the things that first attracted me to Jean Follain's poetry, along with my admiration for all the virtuosic elements of line and syntax that I will talk about in due course, was its simple conjunction of people and places. The places were often foreign to me, removed in both space and time from my actual experience; the people often oddly one-dimensional, at least at first glance; and yet both the people and the places were also strangely familiar. One example: there is a town in one poem, "at the bottom / of a cold fogbound valley," which is noted for producing "knives with blades that open." As I grew to know more about France, this town lost some of its sheen of magical realism and the poem became more documentarian. Such towns did and do exist — Laguiole, Nontron. But this passage also recalled for me Stone-Age villages, such as the one depicted in Jim Crace's fine novel *A Gift of Stones*, that specialized in making sharp-edged tools and blades. Less far back in chronological time, it also reminded me of something I had forgotten from my youth. Among the farms and villages where I grew up one would often find cheese so-called "factories." These were little more that indentations carved into a hillside, with dirt floors and wood- or stone-framed entrances, more often than not, even in my youth, boarded up and no longer operative but still abrupt visual tokens of a once viable artisanal economy like that of the knife-makers.

One sees signs of such an economy throughout Follain's oeuvre and of the people who function, sometimes joyfully, sometimes just barely, in that economy. That is why, when I first read Jean Follain many years ago, I said to myself, "I know these people." No, I did not grow up in Normandy, although, as is the case in Normandy, we did have large apple orchards in and around the villages and rural towns and (eventually) the small urban area where I lived in Wisconsin. Since my father was commander of the local American Legion post, we met many men reminiscing about old wars and the fecklessness of modern youth (as Follain's old men do about draft notices and Napoleanic conflicts). No, the town of my childhood was not destroyed almost completely by bombing (as was St. Lô where Follain went to grammar school, described by Samuel Beckett after the second world war as "The Capital of Ruins," a demarcation that eerily echoes an earlier book of poems from 1926 by Paul Eluard, *Capitale de la Douleur*). In Follain you find men and women fixated on their domestic animals, dogs or cats; you find laborers and property owners alike fixated on their farm animals — obsessed, to use Ted Hughes's fine phrase, "with what horses ail." Where I lived we had horses, although not horse-drawn carriages as in Follain's turn-of-the century landscape — our horses were no longer draft horses. There were

ii

no blacksmiths, no harness-menders who moonlighted as barbers, as in Follain, but my life wasn't far removed from this past. One of my favorite stories my father told was about the way he, as a boy, used to mend leather harnesses in the spring house of the family farm, where the temperature stayed more or less constant year round, warm enough for the leather to be workable in winter, or about grubbing out walnut stumps in the spring that could be turned into rifle butts, a fairly lucrative home economy.

Not just in my parents' day but in mine, too, we gathered morels among oak mulch, wild asparagus along roadways; we had country fairs, feast days, and rural repasts like those in Follain, with strange recluses appearing out of nowhere along with an alien (at least to us small-farming country-folk) part-time population (in our case these were Spanish-speaking migrant workers). One household in Follain has "coal shovels and branding irons," and my father shoveled coal from a bin in our basement that was replenished every month or so with great noise and dirt and excitement. My dad's work bench held tools and farm implements from the last century, just as my mother's kitchen collected old utensils and pans, ones that she still used but that you now see only in museums (or in the bottom cupboards of my kitchen). Her stoves were no longer wood-burning by the time I came on the scene (although she still wrung out laundry the old-fashioned way with an upright roller, washing it on a rubbing board and drying it on indoor lines), but the description of the woman in Follain's poem whose "cast-iron stove" was "as well-maintained as an altar" certainly captures the ambience of my mother's domestic space. The kitchen garden that she maintained when we lived in the country was a quarter of an acre in size, which she mainly plowed and weeded herself, and when I attended the local one-room school (in the wonderfully named Auroraville), I sat at those same desks that the carefree, doomed boys in Follain's poem learn to plot and thieve behind, desks carved with initials, sometimes embellished in colors, that are themselves part of my own viscera.

All of this is to say that there can be a level of nostalgia in looking at Follain's representations of a mainly rural, mainly superceded, life but not mere nostalgia, if that word means a desire to recapture or restore the past. I believe that what Wallace Stevens calls the "motive for metaphor" is in these poems much closer to a wish to understand or at least to articulate what has been lost, not for the sake of the past but for "the future's centuries [that] await," as one poem puts it. Indeed, at this distance, these landscapes peopled with natives, or natives who are returning, or relatives of these natives, or utter strangers—all nursing secret histories, some political, some private—look as alien in the duration or *l'étendue*, to use Follain's word, of my own life, which began in the middle of the twentieth century, as they must have seemed to Follain when he wrote these poems about the same time I was born, himself by then no longer a provincial *normand* but a noted jurist and man-of-letters living in Paris and married to the daughter of two leading painters of the period, Maurice Denis and Madeleine Dinès.

❧　❧　❧

More than a dozen years ago, when I was teaching in Paris as a *professeur invité* at the Sorbonne nouvelle, I was surprised by how little attention Follain was accorded by the academic world, at least by that fragment with which I was conversant. And again back in the States, I learned that he is not routinely taught in modern French poetry classes. Of course as a poet and scholar I am well aware of how work that moves us deeply and has resonance for our own personal histories may not have the scholastic cachet, textual complexity, authorial notoriety, friendships, or influences—whatever—to be actually studied in classrooms instead of just being admired. (A list of apposite English-language writers comes immediately to mind.) Unfamiliar as I was at the time with modern French poetry criticism, however, I wondered if there was more at stake here than the usual professional insouciance. Here is what I, still far from expert in these matters, surmise.

Jean Follain was not designated by Jean-Pierre Richard's mid-century canon-making volume *Onze études sur la poésie moderne* (1964) as one of those eleven germinal poets of modernity. If Follain's reputation in professional French letters did eventually recover, it was never quite completely. He became, to use Robert Frost's metaphor, "a diminished thing"— a minor poet—although his enthusiasts have never gone away, and in some circles even carry the day. For instance, any look at Follain's reception history has to account for his ongoing popular appeal among non-academics. Many ordinary French people, for example, know Follain poems by heart, as they will know, say, poems by Jacques Prévert, and for many of the same reasons. Take, for instance, this early (1933) poem of Follain's, "L'épicier" ("The Greengrocer").

> *L'épicier époux de l'épicière,*
> *avec sa serpillière*
> *et ses doigts de crabe laineux*
> *vend des pois chiches*
> *à la saison pluvieuse*
> *et puis ces grains de riz des Carolines*
> *dents d'Andalouse,*
> *et puis la pipe en sucre rouge,*
> *qui dans la ville où la bâtisse croît,*
> *transfigure*
> *l'enfant à capuchon de crépuscule.*

> The greengrocer
> husband of the other greengrocer
> with his wet mop
> and wooly crab fingers
> sells chickpeas
> in the rainy season
> and later the Carolina rice
> Andalusian teeth,
> and later the red sticks of sugar cane,
> and so the child
> of this town of lengthening buildings
> beams
> beneath dusk's cowl.

The diction is simple but the sounds are playfully intricate (as in the child of the last line — *à capuchon de crépuscule*); its repetitive syntax and unproblematic lineation make the poem easy to memorize; and the poem ends with a complex and magical image of the lengthening shadows at dusk and the little boy, who has grown up eating the greengrocer's seasonal produce, transfigured into a figure out of the past — resembling at once both a new-born with a caul and a ghostly twilit monk under a cowl (although this double-image may be in the French, the pun of course is not). But this slightly archaic, slightly ghostly figure is set against a Fritz Lang-like futuristic scene in which the lengthening shadows of the buildings foreshadow an ominous urban tumescence that will terminate mom-and-pop groceries forever.

In America Follain has enjoyed several brief moments of fame, fuelled initially by W.S. Merwin's translation of his selected poems in 1969, completed several years after the first and only visit made by Follain, a self-confessed xenophobe, to the United States. And then, five years after Follain's untimely death in 1971, Charles Simic and Mark Strand included him in their influential 1976 anthology, *Another Republic,* a selection of "the best European and South American poets and fabulists" who, for the most part, were "not terribly well known," as the editors explained in their preface.

The Simic-Strand anthology, which relied upon the Merwin translations exclusively, seemed to spawn a cottage industry of Follain translation. In 1979 Mary Feeney and William Matthews collaborated on selected "prose poems" by Follain; then in 1981 Louise Guiney translated with the help of Follain's widow his charming memoir of his boyhood, *Canisy,* and in that year Heather McHugh also translated in its entirety the last book of poetry which Follain saw through to the publication stage, *D'après tout*; and finally, in 1985, Feeney and Guiney did a volume called *Selected Prose* for a short-lived press in Durango, Colorado. These publications, and a couple even more out-of-the way editions, were Follain's fifteen minutes of fame in

English. All the translations except McHugh's were by small presses, and all, including McHugh's, are now out of print. Even Merwin's volume of selected translations, originally published by Atheneum, was long out of print and only recently reissued by another small press, Copper Canyon. Except for this 2003 reissue of a 1969 volume, Follain's writing is not now available in North America, and no volume of his poetry has ever been available in English translation in Great Britain.

And yet, in a not-too-distant issue of *Poetry* devoted to "Contemporary French Poetry in Translation" (October/November 2000), the scholar John Taylor notes that a dominant thematic and imagistic focus in contemporary French poetry is "'humble' everyday objects, landscapes, and locales," and he goes on to cite "the great, still insufficiently acknowledged precursor in this domain, Jean Follain (1903-1971)."*

McHugh's translations in 1981 added one critical dimension to Merwin's previous translation work on Follain. She correctly intuited that the key to Follain's aesthetic was not the individual poem but the individual volume of poetry, and she chose as the book in which to represent what I would call Follain's serial

*While the present book was in preparation, at least the British neglect of Follain was partly addressed through two volumes produced by the Anvil Press of London. Neither is a translation of a complete book by Follain; both are anthologies – the first, a collection of "Modern French Poetry, 1938-2008" that begins with a selection of Follain as both poet and essayist (*Into the Deep Street*, edited and translated by Jennie Feldman and Stephen Romer); the second, a selection of poems from across Follain's entire career, all translated by Christopher Middleton.

lyricism the last volume that Follain completed, *D'après tout* (Paris: Gallimard, 1969), whose title she rather oddly chose not to translate. The problem, I would say, is that this is the wrong book to use as the *one* book to represent Follain's work as a lyric poet. It comes late in his career, in the wake of the greatest international recognition he would ever enjoy. Many of these later poems are reworkings of earlier poems, using the same images, sometimes the same implicit narratives, and often the same diction. Yehuda Amichai, the late Israeli poet, confessed that in his own poetry he employed "only a small part of the words in the dictionary," and this is almost pathologically the case with Follain. Follain's earlier volumes obsessively examine, reexamine, turn over, rethread, loop, and project anew a handful of keywords that are vital to the poetic task at hand, but his later volumes perform a similar re-inspection not just of individual words and their nuances but of his own earlier poems. To me, the effect is, as the French would say, *un peu trop fort* or a bit too much (although this effect is felt only if one knows the earlier, more daring poems, and few readers of English do). As a poet Follain always worked on a small canvas, but in my judgment the late lyrics shrink the canvas too preciously, as if he were revising, "after all" (one meaning of *d'après tout*), not his view of the whole world (*tout*) but his view of his own poetry principally.

This shrinkage is in effect the paradoxical and untranslatable meaning in the title of the book, *D'après tout*. To write *d'après* someone is to write in the manner of or even in homage to: the phrase implies imitation. Follain's *tout* I understand as not merely "everything" that is of interest or influence, a meaning that may indeed sound too silly in English to say, but as "all" that has gone before in Follain's own imagination. One might paraphrase the gist, without unkindness, by reshaping it in light of the self-ironic title of one of Paul Verlaine's lyrics: "Follain in the manner of Follain."

So, like McHugh, I have chosen to present Follain through the lens of a single complete volume, but I have chosen what was for Follain a career-making enterprise, his volume of 1953 called *Territoires*, a book that literally and materially makes possible *D'après tout* some fifteen years later. *Territoires*, it ought to be remembered, was published in a seminal year for twentieth-century French poetry in general: it is the year that saw Follain's own publisher, Gallimard, bring out Paul Eluard's posthumous collection (*Poésie ininterrompue II*) as well as the first volume (*Du mouvement et de l'immobilité de Douve*) by a poet who would become one of the major writers of the ensuing generation, Yves Bonnefoy. 1953: it is a watershed year, marking the death of the greatest of the surrealist poets, who was also one of the most politically engaged of the century — Eluard — and the emergence of the postmodern, nonrepresentational, ellipical voice of Bonnefoy, who would become the very opposite of Follain, an international figure as poet, belletrist, and art critic who would teach extensively outside his native country. For Follain, 1953 is the moment when he is just realizing his mature voice.

Follain's *Territoires* is in some ways both a throwback to a more ancient world-vision and the articulation of a new and distinctive, almost ecological, perspective on the human domination of all earthly territories, whether they be of nature, kinship, nationhood, or language. Coming in the wake of the Second World War, Follain's volume often looks back to a world before the First World War, indeed to the world of his turn-of-the-century childhood, rather the way George Eliot's *Middlemarch* reacts to the second Reform Bill in 1871-72 by imagining the world of England fifty years earlier, on the cusp of the first Reform Bill of 1832. But Follain's lyrics do not have narrators as morally assured and tonally stable as Eliot's. His narrators are, both semantically and thematically, much more like the speaker in Thomas Hardy's "In Time of 'The Breaking of Nations,'" a poem written just about the time Jean Follain was born in 1903. Indeed, the third and final stanza of Hardy's poem, with its momentarily archaic diction combined with its fully modern, double-dealing syntax, is a worthy precursor of Follain, perhaps a better one even than any French text:

> Yonder a maid with her wight
> Come whispering by:
> War's annals will fade into night
> Ere their story die.

Even if one is sentimentally disposed to think that the lovers' story will never die, and I suspect some of Hardy's readers might have been, an alternative reading interposes itself, suggesting that *our* twentieth-century wars, far removed as they are from the reference to the Biblical Jeremiah that gives the poem its title, may indeed be apocalyptic enough in their fury that *all* stories will fade into everlasting night. The hint of Keats's "la belle dame sans merci" in the opening line only indicates how far removed from *his* sort of romanticism our own (and Hardy's) "time" is. I am not suggesting that Follain was influenced by Hardy—indeed, during the year that Follain lived in Leeds, because his father thought it would be good for him to go to England, Follain steadfastly refused to learn English. I am noting only that the somewhat incompatible kinds of diction and emotional assumptions made in Hardy's stanza are similar to what one confronts in Follain. Hardy's stylistics can give a non-French reader a textural *feel* for Follain's tonal idiom, as, for instance, in this poem where a child manages to spell out (and presumably read aloud) a conscription notice, prompting this retort from an

old man sipping hard cider
in a blaze of sunshine
[who] says only
"the next century will be worse"
whatever the lovers who pass by are singing.

("The Notice")

For Follain, *territoires* are precisely what the two world wars destroyed. In English the word "territories" implies wildernesses, frontiers—what Huck so idiomatically "lights out for." In Follain's French the word implies regions, yes, and geographical domains—it chronicles colonial units and anticipates the catastrophes of imperial expansion (that conscription notice in the poem quoted above appears "under the N and eagle of Empire")—but it also speaks warmly of kinship groups, of places in which a common language or dialect is spoken. Pablo Neruda has a poem ("No Hay Olvido") that asks, *"Por qué tantas regiones, por qué un día / se junta con un día?"* One could translate this as "Why are there so many regions? What connects / One day to another?" just as one could translate Follain's *territoires* as "regions." But Ben Bellitt's version of Neruda's rhetorical questions is more apposite to what I am saying about Follain's usage. Bellitt in effect paraphrases *regiones* into English: "Why the distinctions of place?" The point that the translator of the Spanish makes is that the term is not literal; the question is not why there are regions but why spaces are demarcated the way they are. That is, what sorts of mapping, whether actual, historical or part of a larger imaginary, confirm, and in some sense *create*, regions? Herein lie Follain's central thematic concerns.

Again and again Follain's book indirectly discloses that *territoires* are what the new homogenizing, postwar French Republic would obfuscate both within France itself and without (in Indochina, say)—that is, the "distinctions of place" in language, in cuisine, and in social and cultural memory. Therefore, I have translated *Territoires* as "Demarcations," recalling the signifying system of mapmakers and discoverers but remembering also that as a technical term in French usage *territoires* signifies areas within the internal anatomy of the human body. George Steiner once speculated that the reason we have so many languages in the world is because language is not primarily for communication but for demarcating and maintaining difference between speakers, and I think that such demarcated differences—their causes and consequences—are precisely the subjects of Follain's book. As one small instance of such "difference," every time a "press" is mentioned in Follain's book, the word signifies a cider press, recalling his native Normandy and not, as for the rest of France, a wine press.

Demarcations is, moreover, first and foremost a war book—not a book about war but one obsessed with the implications for history of postwar worlds; more *Odyssey*, therefore, than *Iliad*. Responding in effect to the politicians who redrew the national boundaries of Europe in 1945 after France's liberation, as much as to those who arbitrarily realigned western European topography in 1815 after the great French defeat at Waterloo, Follain's volume wants to trace its own version of what he imagines to be, in the poem "Police," "the long labor" *(le long travail)*, the essentializing work of ordering and cataloguing relegated to all policing authorities—linguistic, social, or artistic—who try

> by night and day
> with rule and compass
> and colored ink
> to demarcate the entire world.

Cerner, translated here as " to demarcate," literally means to enclose or encircle or even lay siege to (*cerner* is also what you do to the shell of a nut to get the meat out). Here, though, I imagine it in the sense that William Blake in "London" speaks of "each charter'd street" near the "charter'd Thames"—a world (*monde* is Follain's word) which is, we might say, "on the grid," where the "grid" is how all energy is authorized, controlled, and distributed. For Follain the long labor of these enclosing acts of demarcation is virtually synonymous with human endeavor (a number of poems are about labor, both work and child-birth, the gendered activities in which, traditionally, human life is materialized), just as virtually all his poems are, as the distinguished poet Philippe Jaccottet has forcefully pointed out, of the nature of fables.

McHugh argues that Follain's poetry is all "of the moment," for, as she points out, most of his poems are in the present tense. This is factually true but slightly misleading logically. The present is also the tense of much historical narrative and, as a kind of optative subjunctive, it may be also the tense of futural projection. Follain's "time" may be more mythic than strictly documenting the present moment. What I am suggesting is that we have not yet been able to judge the full extent of Follain's lyric triumph because we have not had available in English his widest-ranging, most materialist books.

Territoires itself begins with a poem, narrated in the present tense, called "L'étendue," a complex word in French which can mean *extent, scope, size, area, expanse, range* (as in a singer's vocal range) or even *duration*, as in the expression "l'étendue de la vie." The closing poem is entitled "Evénements," another complex word that neutrally means *events* or *occurrences*, but also *consequences* or *outcomes*, and even a *commotion* or *emergency*. They are probably the two most difficult words I had to translate in this volume if I wanted to remain fairly economical in my

English word choice. But the gist of both words is clear. The perspective of the book is the long view, looking at events and their results and the results of those results in the ongoing expanse or vista of human labor and experience, the "achievement of life itself," as he puts it in the last poem.

This "long view" is what I hope my translation of *Territoires* and this accompanying introduction will provide. To me Follain's poetry is deeply imbued with a sense of human history as an incrementally slow process, one perhaps ultimately unconducive to planetary life, although I am pretty sure that the full political and environmental implications of this stance were not clear to readers in 1953, perhaps not even to Follain himself. To put it another way, the rivers and shorelines in Follain's verses are much more predictive of what our actual dessicated and despoiled twenty-first-century rivers and shorelines look like than Bonnefoy's River Douve is. Yet Follain maintains his visionary aim or apocalyptic accomplishment not by means of prophetic jeremiad but by one of the quietest and most imagistically understated voices that we possess in modern letters. One hears the quietness, so to speak, in "L'épicier," the poem I quoted earlier, in which the image of urban expansion happens so delicately under the veil, as it were, of twilight's ordinarily elongated shadows that it is possible to miss how the future's *supermarché* looms for this greengrocer and his wife.

It is also one of the quiet ironies of Follain's life, given his concern with history, that he was killed in a pedestrian accident in the Place de la Concorde, site of the guillotine at the period when France entered the modern world of radical politics and totalitarianism—run over by an automobile, an object which Follain himself said epitomized all that was wrong with the modern world.

Quiet lyric voices—what the American poet Donald Justice has dryly called "the minor voices"—are always the most difficult to hear. We still have not fully heard in English the Follain that I most value, the vital, essential Follain as identified, say, by the physicist-turned-cultural-theorist Gaston Bachelard, who praised Follain in the early 1950s (or at about the time he was compiling the poems for *Territoires*) as the only French poet to attain what Bachelard celebrated as the "material image"—that is, a poetic image which discloses the authentic materiality of the spatial/temporal continuum in which the self lives. Writing in 1952, or just at the time that *Demarcations* was being completed, the critic Jean Rousselot cited Follain along with Guillevic and Francis Ponge as the three practitioners of a new *poésie matérialiste*. And André Dhôtel, whose 1956 critical introduction to Follain's life and work has never been out of print in France, agrees in effect with the critics named above in seeing *Territoires* as the crux to Follain's poetics and aesthetic vision.

Formally, it is at the level of syntactic invention and lyric compression that Follain makes one of his greatest contributions. Stylistically, his poems depend upon a new way of apportioning the individual verse line through a virtually unpunctuated ordering of words whose meaning the line-breaks disrupt as often as they ratify. The longest poem in *Demarcations* is seventeen lines in length. (I haven't counted the number of lines in *all* of Follain's poetry, but on any given page there is always a sea of white space around the printed text.) The poems use a "purposely limited and purist vocabulary almost without compound adjectives, [foreign] words, or dialect and popular… images." They do, however, use "terms from the world of business, law, the army." "There are few newly coined words." The poet employs a vocabulary "that is very restricted, even commonplace" and "most sparing with superlatives." These lyrics create a "mosaic of words, in which every word, by sound, by placing, and by meaning, spreads its influence to the right, to the left, and over the whole." The game that I have silently introduced here by means of quotation marks has as its only rule that none of these quotations originally applied to Follain …or to any other twentieth-century poet. Except for the last quotation, which comes from Nietzsche, the rest are by the classical scholar David Armstrong, and all describe the odes of Horace. My point is that no modern poet better fits the

Horatian description of a constrained diction with a spatialized, exfoliating syntax than Follain.

My further point in playing this affinity-game between poets is that, despite the flurry of American translations of Follain in the early 1980s, we have yet to witness the poet whose imaginative field is not surrealist-inspired. (Of surrealism he said, "*J'ai admire …j'ai essayé, mais ce n'était pas moi*" [I admire it, I've tried it, but it wasn't me].) But nor is Follain's poetry *predominantly* fabulistic or of the nature of non-historical narrative. It is, rather, an imaginative field like Horace's— formally brilliant, indirectly political, explicitly historical, the epitome of the lyrical, and therefore perhaps ineluctably minor, at least when Follain is compared, say, to the political stage presence of someone like Eluard or to the sheer aesthetic magnitude of someone like Bonnefoy, just as Horace always seems minor compared to his contemporaries Virgil and Ovid. Follain's vision—his typical *poème intimiste*, that quintessentially French genre—comes out of a unique sort of ecological consciousness in which the poetic image takes us back to the origins of lyric poetry itself, to the demarcations of what it means to be genuinely minor—that is, in the context of planetary time, to be merely and unalterably human.

– *Kurt Heinzelman*

ACKNOWLEDGMENTS

Working with Follain's texts over the years, I have learned how these apparently simple poems can produce widely different interpretations and diverse renderings when they have to cross over into English. And so my first debt is to the past translators of Follain who are named in the Introduction. I am especially indebted as well to Jean-Pierre Cauvin, not only for his help with some of these poems and with the act of translation but for his brilliance as an interpreter of French poetry in general. Although Christopher Middleton and I have never discussed our versions of Follain—indeed, I did not know he was translating Follain until I saw his book advertised as forthcoming—he is for me the very model of the poet/translator. I have learned much from his practice in both areas over the years.

I am particularly grateful to my former dissertation student Eliana Schonberg for her assistance early on; to Andrew Cooper, for looking at an earlier draft; to Heather McHugh, for a supportive comment that came at just the right time; to Joe Bratcher for patiently persevering; and to my colleague Karen Pagani for critical insights and inspired guidance in the later stages of preparation. And as always, thank you, Sue, not merely (merely!) for your love and support, but for not letting me forget the necessity of those "acts of attention" that DHL's poetry, and indeed Follain's writings, exemplify. And also for your brilliant translation of Plucky Ducky into a solace for our twelve-year-old that harsh Parisian winter when this project began and nearly died aborning.

DEMARCATIONS

L'ÉTENDUE

Miroitant comme la peau
d'une bête sauvage
le haut chapeau de soie
d'un homme
reste sur son crâne étroit
une femme demeure à son bras
autour d'eux les chantiers à houille
et les tas de sable
peuplent l'étendue exsangue
du paysage de leur vie
mais un écolier étudie
algèbre et géométrie
dans une pièce neutre
et toute blanche.

THE BIG PICTURE

Scintillant
as a wild beast's pelt
a man's shot silk
top hat sits
unmoving
atop his head
a woman
clings to his arm
all around them
coal faces slag
heaps people
the depleted landscape
of their lives
while a boy learns
algebra and geometry
in a room of his own
that is quite white.

LES IMAGES

Un enfant qu'on soulève un peu
un vin foncé
des feuilles tressées en couronnes
un corps vibrant
jusqu'au plus doux aveuglement
n'imposent parfois
aucun désir de dénouement
mais forment dans les yeux
d'éphemères images
qu'on se remémore
au crépuscule
à bruyères noires.

THE IMAGES

A child you try to buck up
an opaque wine
leaves plaited into a crown
a body in the throes
of the sweetest blindness
take shape every now and then
and without the least need to be made sense of
flicker before your eyes
like images recalled
on a black heath
at nightfall

HUMAINS

Des hommes bruns ou blonds
noirs ou rouges
ont pris par un chemin glacé
on veut les revoir ils sont morts.
Par ces temps douteux de pays tempérés
ils firent voir
dans une éclaircie
un bijou d'argent ou d'or
alors qu'ils regardaient les prés
ou quelque village d'abeilles
rappelant les huttes gauloises
à l'écolier fiévreux
qu'ils tenaient ferme par la main.

HUMAN KIND

Men with blond hair or brown
red or black
have passed down this icy road
how one wants to see them again they are dead.
In the changeable weather of these temperate climes
they made a jewel appear
through a break in the clouds
silver or gold
while they gazed at the meadows
or at some village of bees
that looked like the huts of the Gauls
to the feverish schoolboy
they held firmly by the hand.

DURÉES

Le voile étendu sur la tête
quand cet homme
photographiait son fils imberbe
les gens disaient déjà
qu'il était sur le bord
de sa tombe
des femmes cherchaient l'herbe
pour des lapins sans voix
puis venaient les douces vendanges
l'anthracite flambait
dans ces grandes demeures
où parfois du sang noir séchait
près d'une pièce d'or.

CONTINUITIES

The veil stretched all the way over
the head of the man
as he was photographing his smooth-faced son
already people were talking
he was at death's door
already
women pored through the grass
for the rabbits without a voice
then came the late harvest so sweet
the anthracite blazed up
in the great houses
where sometimes blood dried black
beside a clot of gold.

LES LIVRES ET L'AMOUR

Les livres dont s'emplit la chambre
comme des harpes éoliennes s'émeuvent
quand passe le vent venu des orangers
et la lettre dans la page incrustée
se retient
au blanc papier de lin
et la guerre au loin tonne
dans cet automne flamboyant
tuant la maîtresse avec l'amant
au bord d'un vieux rivage.

BOOKS AND LOVE

The books filling up the bedroom
stir the way aeolian harps do
whenever the wind visits from the orange groves
and the letter on the encrusted page
bites into
the white rag paper
and war thunders in the distance
and autumn bursts into flames
killing the beloved along with her lover
where a shoreline used to be.

ÉCOUTER

Il y a ce qui rassure
et dort au cœur de la chose
on l'écoute
dans la boucle du fleuve
dans la houille éclairant
de ses brasiers
le corps de la jeune fille
qui s'expose à la vie
dans la ramure et le jour clair
ou dans la nuit poignante.

LISTENING

Something that comforts us
sleeps at the heart of the thing
we listen to it
when a river turns back on itself
when a blast from the furnace lights up
a young girl laying her whole body
open to life
under the foliage
in broad daylight
or the poignant dark.

L'INNOCENCE

A l'école on répétait
le problème
de l'étoffe et de la citerne
et sur la route personne
hormis l'homme à blouse soutachée
se désaltérant aux fontaines
dans sa poche tintaient des sous
du même bronze que les cloches
mais dans l'été la pianiste
entamait ce vieil air
innocentant le monde.

INNOCENCE

Over and over at school
you studied the problem
of substance and hydraulics
and along the way no one stopped
to quench his thirst at any fountain
except for the man in the corded overalls
coins jingling in his pocket
same brass as the bells
but in summer the piano player
struck up that old tune
absolving the world of its wrongs.

VIE DES CAMPAGNES

Une renoncule âcre appelée
bouton d'or
un matin est simplement cueillie
l'arbre n'en frémit pas d'autant
les insectes constructeurs
tournent autour
et ils sont cuirassés
ils ont des yeux à facettes
et portent des armes
minuscules et lancinantes
mais lorsque le sol s'échauffe
les rondes des enfants commencent.

FIELD LIFE

One morning a ranunculus
the bitter kind
called buttercup
is culled just like that
no tree snaps to attention so fast
armor-plated insects
scurry about
the kind with faceted eyes
who are builders
and bear arms
minute yet lacerating
but once the ground gets worked up
out come the children dancing.

FÉLICITÉ

La moindre fêlure
d'une vitre ou d'un bol
peut ramener la félicité d'un grand souvenir
les objets nus
montrant leur fine arête
étincellent d'un coup
au soleil
mais perdus dans la nuit
se gorgent aussi bien d'heures
longues
ou brèves.

BLISS

The least crack
in a bowl or pane of glass
can bring back the sheer bliss of a fine memory
bare things
their fishbone-fine filigree
sparkling in a stroke
of sunlight
but lost at nightfall
swallow the hours whole
the long ones
or the short.

L'ACHETEUSE

Elle achetait un élixir
dans la ville
d'un autre temps
il nous faut penser à elle
encore aujourd'hui pourtant
quand les bras sont aussi blancs
et les poignets aussi fins
aussi douce la chair
ô vertigineuse vie !

THE SHOPPER

She bought a potion
in the city
out of another era
and yet we need to think of her
again today
because of arms so white
wrists so fine
so soft this flesh
oh vertiginous life!

LA BELLE ET LES BÊTES

Quand elle viendra enfin
le cimetière alors sera chaud
et fendillé
le beau sol sec
elle sera entourée
de gémissements de cris
de hurlements d'animaux et d'humains
mais si loin
dans l'étendue
que l'on n'entendra rien
alors elle s'appuiera à l'arbre
et parlera tout habillée
aux bêtes les plus nues
heureusement proches.

BEAUTY AND THE BEASTS

When she finally comes back
the cemetery will be hot
the good earth
dry in fissures
she will be surrounded
by howls and moanings
cries human and inhuman
but so remote
in the big picture
that nothing is heard
she'll prop herself then against a tree
and speak fully clothed
to the animals that are perfectly naked
and glad to be near.

OMBRES ET LUEURS

Dans l'ombrage d'un clos
tout un monde dévore
et l'officier rentre
l'habit chargé de tresses noires
une feuille lobée
tremble au vent du nord
tenant le bois de table
d'une main carrée
résiste un homme
qu'entourent ses abeilles
mais la femme
émiette un pain friable
au cercle des oiseaux bénis.

SHADOWS AND GLIMPSES

In the shadowy light of the farmyard walls
a whole world seems to be gorging itself
pulling on a uniform black with campaign ribbons
the officer re-enlists
a lobate leaf
shakes in the north wind
hands firm
as the table top they hold onto
a man goes on
his bees all about him
while his wife
crumbles her bread away
inside a circle of birds
by way of blessing.

DES FORMES

Des formes se défont
dans un grand tourment
le sang s'évade
de la bête qu'on tue
un peu se fige en elle
mais on transcrit des noms
sur les piliers trapus.
A de certains jours
s'éclairent les villages
et les villes captieuses
un visage apparaît
dominant un corps de jeunesse
marchant au pied de vieux remparts.

FORMS

They come undone
in one great agony
blood escapes
from the slain beast
a bit of it clotting
but names are transcribed
onto the stout pillars.
Some days the villages are lit up
and the specious towns
a face appears
lording it over a corps of young people
walking at the foot of ancient battlements.

CHEVELURES

A l'approche des nuits
et dans les ports de guerre
on voit des chevelures
apparaître étagées
et longuement lavées
de femmes qui tiennent
dans leurs bras des enfants
ou qui chantent ou qui tremblent
ou finement répondent
pas une lueur ne bouge
sur les architectures.

HAIR STYLES

As each night comes on
and in every port of war
one sees them
backbrushed wet and layered
in storeys
belonging to women who hold
children in their arms
who sing or tremble
or answer deftly
not a speck of light musses
this architecture.

PAROLES

On parlait d'amours prétendues
à l'ancienne table
où travaillaient les vers
sur le fourneau le fer chauffait
la lentille cuisait sombre
par la porte ouverte
la beauté du feuillage amer
et des oiseaux à gorge rouge
devant les mots humains
que gouvernait une syntaxe éprouvée
resplendissait.

WORDS

Loves so-called
were spoken of
around the antique table
where worms had burrowed
the fire warmed the stove
simmering lentils darkened
through an open doorway
facing human words
that mastered a well-worn syntax
the beauty of the bitter foliage
and the red-throated birds
dazzled.

LES AMIS

Au début du siècle
ils étaient là lançant le rire cruel
entre des murs de chaux
sauvagement mordant
à ces pommes de glace
d'un verger de collège
et se livrant au vol
dans les pupitres clos
éclaboussés par l'encre.
C'était dans une cité
qui s'engloutirait dans les flammes
mais bien après leur mort
survenue au cœur d'un été vaste.

THE FRIENDS

At the turn of the century
they were hurling barbs of laughter
among the whitewashed walls
biting savagely
into the frozen apples
in the school orchard
and then they studied theft
behind their closed
ink-besplattered desktops.
This was in an old part of town
that would be swallowed up in flames
though well after death
caught them out
at the heart of an endless summer.

ABSENCE

Le métal fond pour se marier à l'air
et la consolation
abandonne un homme
caressant l'encolure
d'un cheval de labour
qui regarde
un horizon au froid plumage.
On voit un filet de fumée
une feuille qui s'envole
seul l'homme est obligé de sentir la durée.

ABSENCE

Metal melting weds itself to air
and the power to comfort
deserts a man
stroking the neck
of a draft horse
as he keeps on eye on
the frigid plumage of the horizon.
There's a streak of smoke
a leaf swirling off
and man alone who is forced to feel
how things go on.

TOUTE LA BEAUTÉ

Les animaux courent on dirait sans but
la fille fraîchement lavée
a sur eux son regard
comme au monde
elle arrive tard
n'ayant appris à l'école
à peu près rien
et pourtant qui connaît l'histoire
des siècles impurs
reportera sur elle vénuste et blanche
toute la beauté.

BEAUTY ITSELF

Animals rush about it is said without any purpose
so the fresh scrubbed girl
regards them
as the world does
a view she is late coming to
having learned at school
next to nothing
and yet those familiar with history
the centuries of turpitude
will ascribe to her
beauty itself
zaftig and perfectly white.

RIVAGES

On voit des figures pâles
près des maisons anciennes
un soldat d'autrefois
une femme empruntée
qui marche à ses côtés
par un jour sans visage
tout près d'eux
l'océan se retire
laissant le coquillage strié
ébréché près du galet gris
une voiture emplie de varech
rentre avec la nuit fidèle à l'exilé
qui porte en sautoir sa jumelle marine.

SHORELINES

One sees their wan shapes
near the oldest houses
a soldier time has passed by
a woman walking
ill-at-ease beside him
featureless as the day itself
up close to them
the sea withdraws
leaving a gray striated necklace
of broken shells
a chariot full of sea-wrack
returns with the night
keeping faith with the exile
who wears round his neck
his watery twin.

AU PAYS

Ils avaient décidé de s'en aller
au pays
où la même vieille femme
tricote sur le chemin
où la mère
secoue un peu l'enfant
lui dissant à la fin des fins
te tairas-tu, te tairas-tu ?
Puis dans le jeu à son amie
la fillette redit tu brûles
et l'autre cherche si longtemps
si tard – ô longue vie –
que bientôt les feuilles sont noires.

TO THE COUNTRY

They had decided to go off
to the country
where the same old woman
is knitting by the side of the lane
where the mother
shakes her child a little
and says for the umpteenth time
will you hush now hush now?
And then in the game the little girl
again calls out you're getting warmer
and her friend's looking for so long
so late — oh such long life —
that soon the leaves are black.

L'ATLAS

Presque femme une fillette
lavait
un linge à dentelles et jours
au fleuve gravé finement
dans l'atlas qu'emportait
un fils de la vallée
vers la ville aux tours penchées
et sous son bras déjà fort
sans rien regarder des arbres
il tenait farouchement
les figures du monde entier.

THE ATLAS

A young girl nearly a woman
was doing the wash
of linen hemstitched lace-bordered
in a river a finely etched line
in the atlas
carried up from the valley
to the town of slanted towers
by a young man
who never once glanced at the trees
under his arm already so strong
he held fiercely onto
all the illustrations of the world.

GLACE ROUGE

L'an mil huit cent douze en Russie
quand les soldats faisaient retraite
au milieu de cadavres
d'hommes et de chevaux
avait gelé le vin robuste
la hache du sapeur
dut alors partager
entre tous même moribonds
le bloc de glace rouge
à forme de futaille
qu'aucun musée
n'eût pu jamais garder.

RED ICE

In the year eighteen twelve in Russia
with the soldiers in retreat
amidst corpses
of men and of horses
the hearty wine froze
the axe of the sapper
in those days had to parse out
all manner of things
even the dying
the barrel shaped
block of red ice
no museum on earth
could ever preserve.

TRAGIQUE HIVER

Plus de berger à l'horizon
s'appuyant sur le roc à fleurs minuscules
on balayait les maisons
des familles silencieuses
dont les filles à corsage étroit
au visage strictement nu
avec des bâillements montraient
le rose de leur palais
peu soucieuses d'une beauté
attachée aux mêmes rivages.

TRAGIC WINTER

Scarcely a shepherd left on the horizon
leaning on a rock aflower
houses were swept
belonging to silent families
with daughters in tight bodices
their stern faces unrouged
whose yawns showed
rosy palates
and little concern for a beauty
tied to shores like theirs.

L'ASSIETTE

Quand tombe des mains de la servante
la pâle assiette ronde
de la couleur des nuées
il en faut ramasser les débris,
tandis que frémit le lustre
dans la salle à manger des maîtres
et que la vieille école ânonne
une mythologie incertaine
dont on entend
quand le vent cesse
nommer tous les faux dieux.

THE PLATE

When the plate falls from the servant's hand
round and pale
the color of clouds
the pieces do have to be picked up,
the whole time the chandelier trembles
in the masters' dining room
while the old school goes on droning its recitations
of a mythology
fleeting but still heard
when the wind stops
calling by name every false god.

VOYAGEUSES

Elles frémissaient dans leurs lombes
des feuilles tourbillonnaient
sur celle fixe d'un houx
restait la goutte de sang
qu'une main égratignée
y avait laissée intacte.
Dans les maisons citadines
s'étendait sur les paliers
un silence mortifié
mais, d'un embonpoint gracieux
vêtues en robes immenses
un landau les emportait.

WOMEN TRAVELLING

Cramps stitched their lumbar regions
leaves swirled
a holly bough scarcely moved
after a scratched hand left behind on it
droplets of blood.
On every landing through all the housing
in the city
mortified silence
but they were borne along
their noble stoutness draped
by lavish dresses
in a light carriage.

LE VOLEUR DE FAUX

Il fuit par des sentiers
avec la faux volée
tout près dans une serre
s'ouvre la sensitive
dans la plaine nue
bouge
la maison du berger.
Voleur si petit aux regards de ceux-là
montés sur une tour
à créneaux d'autrefois
qui contemplent la mer
pour croire au bonheur
et tuer le temps bavard
jusqu'au beau soir !

THE THIEF OF SCYTHES

He flees on foot
with the stolen scythe
nearby in a greenhouse
a sensitive plant
opens
a shepherd's hut
on a featureless plain
is stirring.
Such a petty thief in the eyes of those
looking on from a tower
crenellated in the old way
who muse at length upon the sea
so as to believe in happiness
and shoot the breeze
until the lovely dusk!

LES ENFANTS

Les enfants jouent au théâtre
jusqu'à l'heure
du souper dans la nuit qui vient
alors les grandes personnes les appellent
le garçon a les yeux si clairs
puis voici celle qui mourra jeune
et celle dont sera seul le corps
tous se lavent les mains dans l'ombre
près des végétaux flamboyants
et sont encore dans ce temps
que l'on vit dans l'éternité.

THE CHILDREN

The children play at their play-acting
right until nightfall
the supper hour
when the grownups call them in
the boy has eyes so clear
and the girl who will die young
is here and the one
whose body will always be lonely
all wash their hands
in shadow
in the shade of such extravagant vegetation
and are again inside the time
which is the one one lives forever.

CALOMNIE

Dans cette ville où le haras s'effrite
où pèle un mur d'hospice
la cheminée
comme un guignol de cendres
la pelle à feu
et le dernier tison
sont témoins de flancs purs,
d'un cœur calomnié
dans la détresse obscure.

SLANDER

In this town where the stud pens
are falling down
where a hospital wall peels away
the chimney
like a puppet of ash
the coal shovel and the last branding iron
bear witness to unmarked flanks,
to a slandered heart
inexplicably distraught.

OISEAUX

Ramasse la plume cendrée
enfant terreux
à l'ombre rouge
le bourg cuit dans le feu du soleil
le cœur des bois
palpite d'oiseaux fins
ils ne regrettent pas
la couronne ou le haut casque à la Minerve
passant autrefois sous les branches
ne revoient-ils pas les troupeaux
devant les eaux taries
le mariage des branches
une biche alertée ?

BIRDS

Gather the ashen feather
country boy
in the red shade
a town is baking in the sun
the heart of the woods
pulses with exquisite birds
they do not regret
laurel crowns or tall Minervan helmets
passing in bygone days under the boughs
can't they see
the herds trooping again to dried-up springs
the wedlock of limbs
a doe poised to flee?

FINESSE D'UN JOUR

Que sur les seuils
se montrent des visages
on voit aussi des mains jeter une eau fumante
et l'on entend des bêtes
soupirer dans des doigts d'ouvrier.
Cependant par-delà les jardins construits
aux plantes balancées
mais qui serrent leurs graines
se nouent les vapeurs
se rejoignent les plaintes.

A DAY'S REFINEMENT

When at the thresholds
faces appear
one also sees jets of steam
shooting through hands
and hears animals sighing
under the workman's fingers.
Nearby though are well-built gardens
of well-matched plants
but they store away their seeds
knit vapors
entwine laments anew.

BIENVENUE

Dans la ferme rechampie
c'est un jour soleilleux
que l'on attend l'étranger.
Vêtu de drap noir et fin
et coiffé du chapeau haut
il va pousser la barrière
et dire amis me voici.
L'âne broutant le chardon bleu
la jument en robe sombre
le porc buveur de lait maigre
le chien au front étoilé
le chat sensible aux orages
devant lui seront les mêmes
qu'en la dure Antiquité.

WELCOME

On the newly painted farm
it's a sunshiny day
as they wait for
the one from Away.
Dressed in black worsted
fine as his silk hat
he pushes the gate open
says look friends I'm here.
The ass nibbling blue thistles
the mare in her winter coat
the pig drinking thin milk
the dog with a star on the forehead
the cat who is spooked by storms
gather before him the same
as in the hardness of Antiquity.

FRATERNITÉS

Quand le voleur de voitures
rencontre le voleur de chevaux
ils mangent lentement,
la sauce dans leurs assiettes à fêlures
doucement se fige
ils voient dans la brume
la statue équestre de la place
près des étriers de granit
plus grands que nature
des couples échangent
leurs mots clairs.

BROTHERHOODS

When the thief of horses
meets the thief of carriages
they eat slowly
the sauce has time to congeal
in the cracks of their dinner plates
they look through the mist
toward the equestrian statue in the square
where under granite stirrups
larger than life
a few couples exchange
their own clear words.

HABITUDES

Dans une vie difficile
elle enlevait au capitaine
ses épaulettes à torsades
pour le regarder dans les yeux
on entendait parfois sonner
le clairon d'un poste d'alarme
le vent emportait l'odeur fauve
mais le fourneau de fonte restait
entretenu comme un autel
il y tombait une larme.

PRACTICES

In a life of difficulty
she stripped from his captain's uniform
the finely embroidered epaulettes
so she could look him better in the eyes
they heard alarms at times
bugled from the garrison
wind bore the stink of cat
but her cast-iron stove
as well-maintained as an altar
stayed right where it was
whenever a tear fell.

CONTOURS

Barbier à ses heures
le bourrelier rasait
tout restait sinueux
en lui et ses entours
sa grande barbe fourchue
ses colliers pour chevaux
et les torsades des brandebourgs
sur le dolman du hussard,
son fils qui sur un seuil brisé
restait tout prêt
pour d'autres temps.

CONTOURS

The harness maker
a barber at other times
gave shaves and trims
everything in and around him
stayed tightly wound
his great forked beard
the collars for his horses
and the Brandenburgian brocades
on the hussars' jackets,
his son stood still at a cracked sill
more than ready
for times to change.

LA MORT

Avec les os de bêtes,
l'usine avait fabriqué ces boutons
qui fermaient
un corsage sur un buste
d'ouvrière éclatante
lorsqu'elle tomba
l'un des boutons se défit dans la nuit
et le ruisseau des rues
alla le déposer
jusque dans un jardin privé
où s'effritait
une statue en plâtre de Pomone
rieuse et nue.

DEATH

The factory made buttons
from animal bones
that fastened the blouse
of one who worked there
a vivacious woman
when she fell down
one night one of those buttons broke off
and a network of streets
streamed it away
to a private garden
where a plaster statue of a goddess
well endowed weathered away
naked laughing.

LA LOTERIE

On a brisé
la petite loterie
où l'on gagnait un verre à fleurs
et des gens restent
autour des débris de sa roue
béats dans leur vêture
jupes roidies et scintillantes
vestes incrustées
de larmes de plâtre
redingotes noires épuisées.
Sous ces hardes les corps parfois beaux
de ceux qui tentèrent pour si peu la fortune
frissonnent au vent de mer.

THE LOTTERY

They broke the pot
for the lottery bets
where winning meant a bud vase
and the people are left
standing among the leftovers from fortune's wheel
gay in their finery
stiff skirts and shiny jackets
encrusted with teardrops of plaster
braids of black trim worn thin.
Beneath these rags are the bodies
occasionally beautiful
of those who laid out so much for so little
shivering in the breeze off the sea.

LA GLACE

Après avoir monté les escaliers
de chêne sombre
elle se trouve devant la glace
au cadre que rongèrent les vers
elle y contemple un torse vierge
toute la campagne est embrasée
et doucement arrive à ses pieds
une bête domestique
comme pour rappeler
cette vie animale
qu'aussi bien recèle
un corps de femme.

THE MIRROR

Having climbed the stairway
of severe oak
she finds herself face to face with the mirror
framed in wood the worms have gnawed at
she sees in it the torso of a virgin
all the countryside put to the torch
and softly at her feet a household pet
materializes
as if to recall what animal life
couches as well
in a woman's body.

CONSPIRATION

Les glaces reflètent
des glaives et trophées
chrétienne elle se défait
de sa robe écumeuse
pleine d'agrafes, de rubans, de nœuds
puis de tout son corps tendu
écoute la vie en elle
mais les âmes
de la conspiration
veillent à travers les piliers
et le cri survenu du porteur d'eau
fait éclater l'or d'un silence païen.

CONSPIRACY

The mirrors reflect
trophies and two-handed swords
a Christian she lets down
her gown of foam
full of hooks, ribbons, knots
then stretching so that her whole body
listens to the life inside her
but the conspiracy
has master-minds
watching round every column
and the sudden cry of the water carrier
shatters into gold a pagan silence.

VIE

Il naît un enfant
dans un grand paysage
un demi-siècle après
il n'est qu'un soldat mort
et c'était là cet homme
que l'on vit apparaître
et puis poser par terre
tout un lourd sac de pommes
dont deux ou trois roulèrent
bruit parmi ceux d'un monde
où l'oiseau chantait
sur la pierre du seuil.

LIFE

A child is born
in a landscape of vistas
half a century later
he is only a dead soldier
and there it was that we saw
this man appear
and set on the ground
a full sack heavy with apples
a few of which rolled out
one noise among others in a world
where a bird went on singing
atop a threshold of stone.

L'ILLUSION

Là vivait l'illusion tenace
des couples chicaneurs
des enfants entraient
réclamant leurs parents
sur un ton sans douleur
on buvait ces boissons
de la couleur des sels du cuivre
et l'amer à l'orange
étincelait au couchant faubourien
pour décor sur le comptoir
où s'étreignaient des mains fugaces
un ange de bronze
souriait figurant la concorde.

THE ILLUSION

Here for couples who liked to quarrel
the illusion persisted
children entering
demanded their parents back
but in voices that felt no pain
they downed their drinks
the color of salt and of copper
and the bitter orange one
twinkled in the bar's blue-collar twilight
like a stage set
where fugitive hands were wrung
and a smiling bronze angel
stood for peace.

LES SIÈCLES

Regardant la marque du sabot
de son cheval de sang
le cavalier dans cette empreinte contournée
où déjà des insectes préparaient leur ouvroir
devina la future imprimerie
puis pour lui demander sa route
il s'approcha du charpentier
qui près d'une rose
en repos contemplait la vallée
et ne lirait jamais de livres.

THE CENTURIES

Looking back at the mark
left by the hoof of his horse
a thoroughbred
in whose undulant impression
insects had already started their needlepoint
the horseman foresaw the coming of moveable type
and then to ask the way
rode up to a carpenter
at rest beside a rosebush
his mind on the valley below
and who would never read a book.

MOYEN AGE

On voit une fleur
lentement s'épanouir
les étains et les clous
épuiser la clarté
un grain de chair à la roue
du supplice rester
et la fille nue
du treizième siècle
de ses seins et de ses bras
lutte contre le temps
près d'une rose de pierre.

MEDIEVAL

A flower is seen to unfold
in slow motion
tin and nails
depleting the clarity
a seed of torn flesh
left over on the wheel
and the naked girl
of the thirteenth century
is struggling with her arms and breasts
against time itself
beside a rose of stone.

DOMAINE D'HOMME

L'homme éternel cultive
son terrain et gémit
sur le temps
pourvoyeur des blés et des vignes
quel cruel soleil un jour
mais quelle douce fraîcheur un autre
à la maison une femme au corps de gloire
met le couvert
un papillon la suit sans fin
rompant le pain
le journalier écoute fuir chaque minute.

MAN'S ESTATE

Man cultivates eternally
his plot of ground and groans
about the weather
purveyor of wheat and vines
what brutal sun one day
but how sweetly cool the next
at home a woman is laying the table
her body a work of glory
a butterfly follows her endlessly
breaking bread
the day-laborer hears each minute flee.

POLICE

D'un bureau de police donnant sur un jardin
près d'une fosse
et d'une serre
le tournant de la route apparaît
orné de sombres ciguës
un oiseau s'y attarde
une fleur s'y penche
et le long travail se poursuit
avec règle et compas
et encre de couleur
qui nuit et jour s'efforce
à cerner le monde.

POLICE

From a police station opening onto a garden
near a dump
and a greenhouse
the bend in the road appears
adorned with dark hemlocks
a bird lingers there
a flower bends
and the long labor is carried on
as best one can
by night and day
with rule and compass
and colored ink
to demarcate the entire world.

LA POUPÉE

La trève des oiseaux siffleurs
annonçait l'orage
d'un livre il voletait une page
près d'une charrue égarée.
Sur l'écorce d'un chêne
front posé sanglotait quelqu'une
étreignant la poupée
maintenant sans bras
achetée aux jours de l'éternelle enfance.
Les ombres étaient démesurées
et le premier coup du tonnerre
fit tressaillir l'amante.

THE DOLL

The truce among whistling birds
signaled the storm
which riffled a page in a book
near a stranded plow.
With forehead pressed to the bark
of an oak tree sobbing
she clasped the doll to her
armless now
bought in the time of endless childhood.
The shadows were out of all proportion
and the first peal of thunder
made this lover tremble.

POISSONS

Les poissons
vus par l'économie
sont abaissés par des mains éplucheuses
grattant l'écaille
scrutant l'œil mort
alors qu'au jardin ploient les tiges
et que l'air pur qui passe
par l'entrebâillement d'une fenêtre
flatte une femme qui se dévêt
et qui jamais n'a vu la mer.

FISH

Fish
according to the market
lose value to the hands that gut them
scraping scales
assessing freshness in dead eyes
but then the stems in the garden bend
with the fresh air passing
through a half-open casement
pleasing a woman who is undressing
and has never seen the sea.

L'ŒUF

La vieille dame essuie un œuf
avec son tablier d'usage
œuf couleur ivoire et lourd
que nul ne lui revendique
puis elle regarde l'automne
par la petite lucarne
et c'est comme un tableau fin
aux dimensions d'une image
rien n'y est
hors de saison
et l'œuf fragile
que dans sa paume elle tient
reste le seul objet neuf.

THE EGG

The old woman wipes the egg clean
with her well-used apron
egg the color of ivory and heavy
nobody can take it back
then she gazes out at the fall
through her high little window
and it's like an elaborate picture
refined to a single image
nothing there
is out of season
and the fragile egg
she holds in her palm
remains the sole new thing.

PENSÉES D'OCTOBRE

On aime bien
ce grand vin
que l'on boit solitaire
quand le soir illumine les collines cuivrées
plus un chasseur n'ajuste
les gibiers de la plaine
les sœurs de nos amis
apparaissent plus belles
il y a pourtant menace de guerre
un insecte s'arrête
puis repart.

THOUGHTS OF OCTOBER

How one savors
this fine wine
when it is enjoyed alone
when evening lights up the coppery hillsides
no hunter takes aim any longer
at the lowland game
the sisters of your friends
seem more beautiful
notwithstanding threats of war
an insect lets up
then's at it again.

LE GLOBE

Tout seul l'écolier d'un village
allait portant au maître
un globe terrestre
tenant en main le piédestal bronzé
et le feu de la forge
éclairait sphère et vin sombrant
dans le gosier des maréchaux
à tablier de peau de chien.

THE GLOBE

All by himself the village schoolboy
carried to the schoolmaster
a globe
one hand holding its bronzed stand
and the fire in the forge
lit up both the sphere and the wine
staining the dark throats of the farriers
in their smocks of dogskin.

FOURMIS NOIRES

Les mains aux poches il regarde
le monde des fourmis noires
leur sang couleur de laque
leurs aiguillons
leurs larves blanches
frémissantes aux vibrations
d'une cloche
son violon de jeune homme dort dans un coffre
et la nuit va semer ses étoiles
sur la carte céleste.

BLACK ANTS

Hands in his pockets he observes
the world of the black ants
lacquer the color of their blood
their mandibles
their white larvae
trembling at the strokes
of a bell
the young man's violin sleeps in its case
and night disseminates its stars
across the celestial charts.

LA POMME ROUGE

Le Tintoret peignit sa fille morte
il passait des voitures au loin
le peintre est mort à son tour
de longs rails aujourd'hui
corsettent la terre
et la cisèlent
la Renaissance résiste
dans le clair-obscur des musées
les voix muent
souvent même le silence
est comme épuisé
mais la pomme rouge demeure.

THE RED APPLE

Tintoretto painted his dead daughter
in the distance carriages were passing
in turn the painter himself died
these days endless rails
corset the earth
they chisel it
the Renaissance lives on
in the chiaroscura of museums
voices break and change
quite often silence itself
sounds depleted
but the red apple is there still.

LA FÊTE

Vérité, imposture
où donc vous cachez-vous ?
Et qui tapisse de silence
les chambres du monde ?
Quand un grand praticien
ausculte le corps étendu
d'une beauté
le colporteur rentre
dans la maison des champs
et dit confusément
des mots tendres à des bêtes
dont c'est alors la fête.

FEAST DAY

Truth, imposture
where are you hiding yourselves?
Who is hanging killims of silence
in the bedrooms of the world?
When an eminent physician
listens for a pulse from the outstretched body
of a pretty woman
the peddler bursts into the little house on the prairie
and speaks a few tender words
confusedly to the animals
whose feast day
this is.

DANS LE TEMPS

Au temps des innombrables suites
du roi Soleil
il avait gelé
une nuit sur la terre
l'homme après boire
avait essuyé sa moustache blonde
et la femme un peu regardé
les cristaux du givre
les siècles futurs attendaient
longue armée
au sommet des monts.

BACK WHEN

In the days of the countless retinues
attending the Sun King
the weather got frigid
one night on the ground
the man after drinking
wiped off his blond mustache
and the woman barely noticed
the crystals of frost
the future centuries were waiting
a standing army
reaching to the mountain peaks.

DES FLEURS

Des fleurs semblent regarder
groupées en nombre
sur les bords d'un ravin
et l'on peut avoir peur de ces touffes
à même le terreau
ne dormant pas,
aucun meunier aucun fardier
mais le seul ciel
d'une province
où parfois un grand bol se casse
à fleurs peintes.

ABOUT FLOWERS

In large clumps
at the edge of a ravine
flowers appear to be watching
and one could come to fear these tufts
nestled in leaf-mold
never dozing,
no miller no haywain
not even lone sky
over the deepest countryside
at those times when a food bowl glazed with flowers
breaks.

HORS DURÉE

Sains et saufs les poissons
oubliés
sont dans l'étang morne
couverts de nuances
les chiens regardent
en témoins de l'homme ;
les frissons du chêne creux
le cri d'un oiseau lointain
sont perçus du cavalier qui rentre
d'une guerre de trente ans.

AFTERMATH

The fish are safe and sound
forgotten
in their turgid pond
crosshatched by shadows
the dogs look on
the man witnesses,
the shudder of the hollow oak
the cry of a bird far off
are all the soldier takes in
as he rides back
from a thirty-years war.

GRAINETIER

Le jour n'est pas fini
et l'homme dort
sous un ciel sans terreur
bientôt il lui faudra porter
le maïs et l'orge
le sarrasin couleur gris de souris
le son rosâtre
puis s'enfoncer par le chemin
avec le dernier sac bossué
d'avoine blême.

SOWER

Day is not over
and the man is asleep
under a sky without fear
soon he will need to carry
the maize and barley
the mousy gray buckwheat
the pinkish bran
then he'll vanish down a lane
humpbacked by a last
sad sack of oats.

LA FEMME ET L'ENFANT TRAVESTIE

Courageuse aux coups destin
un soir de carnaval une femme
par la main tenait une enfant
travestie en folie
les grands monuments s'étendaient
devant leur marche vive
et les grelots sonnaient
sur l'habit mi-partie
rouge et jaune
de la fillette pâle autant que le ciel.

WOMAN AND CHILD IN COSTUME

Braving the strokes of fate
one evening at Carnaval
a woman led by the hand
a child in a ludicrous costume
large public monuments lengthened
before their brisk steps
while the bells jingled
on the motley suit
half-yellow half-red
the little girl wore
herself pale as the sky.

MURAILLE

C'est un moellon violâtre
mal pris dans son ciment
qui se fend sous le gel
mais se tiendra l'ensemble
alors l'homme simple
qui à chaque aurore
tourne la clef dans la serrure
contourne son parterre
jette un os au chien noir
mourra seul collé contre son mur
en voyant des fumées
aux horizons fuyants.

FORTIFIED WALL

It is a violet hewn stone
badly cemented
split by frost
but it will hold together
while the simple man
who turns each dawn
the key in the lock
takes a turn round the flowerbeds
throws a bone to the black dog
will die alone pressed against his own wall
watching smoke swirls
brush away every horizon.

LE PAYSAGE

Cet homme à l'habit sombre
porte aux pieds des bottines hâves
où montent des insectes fins
les moellons de la maison
sont par le dur ciment liés
il grandit le hêtre rouge
le paysage est celui
où se déroulera
une bataille d'étrangers
dont l'air charriera les bruits
dans cette campagne altérée
où tremblent à peine les cimes.

THE LANDSCAPE

This man in dark clothing
is wearing low boots once almost elegant
now minute insects scale them
the stones of the house
are set in rough cement
the red beech grows there
the landscape the one
where foreigners will clash
air churning with battle-noise
in a changed countryside
where mountain peaks barely tremble.

ESPOIR

L'aîné et son cadet
parlent au bord du précipice
au-dessus d'eux des nuées essaiment;
portant un habit d'apparat
une épée
qu'ils ont loués
ils respirent l'odeur des arbres élancés
une brise incline la fleur crucifère;
tout près des salariés descendent aux mines
le plus jeune a devant lui croit-il
au moins un demi-siècle à vivre
il sourit au banal espoir.

HOPE

The older boy and his brother
are speaking at the edge of the precipice
above them some clouds gathering;
wearing the induction robes
and the épée
they have rented
they breathe in the odor of the slender trees
a cruciferous flower nods in the breeze;
workers go down the nearby mines
the youngest has he believes
fifty more years at least in front of him
and is smiling
at such an uninspired aspiration.

MORTE-SAISON

Un homme écoutait l'objection
d'un autre
qui voulait son âme immortelle
sur un seuil de porte une femme
jouait avec une bête
en pleurant
et dans les offices restaient
les végétaux, le lait
les bassines
aux reflets de sang.

OFF-SEASON

One man was listening to the counter-argument
from the other one
who believed his soul immortal
in a doorway a woman
played with an animal
while she wept
and there remained in the sculleries
vegetables and milk
in basins
reflections of blood.

TABLÉES

Dans les entours et sur la table
où la soupe se trempe lentement
les choses
paraissent sans offense
chacun est habillé de drap
mais la femme n'a point de hâle
ils sont tous des mêmes villages
gardés par des chiens hérissés
les couteaux dont les lames s'ouvrent
viennent d'une ville bâtie
au fond d'une vallée à frimas
des astres au-dessus d'eux voyagent
comme le racontent maints ouvrages
parus sur terre
il y a beau temps.

AT TABLE

Nothing anywhere around them
appears to offend
where the soup is cooling slowly on the table
everyone has on homespun
though the woman's skin is without a trace of sun
they are all from the same villages
guarded by the same bristling dogs
the knives with the blades that open
come from a town at the bottom
of a cold fogbound valley
stars sojourn above them
the way it is told in so many works
that came forth on earth
a good long time ago.

PHÉNOMÈNE

Une fille à pelage de bête
était montrée aux badauds
et ceux-ci repartaient
dans le couchant forain
cependant qu'elle
ayant fait sa journée
cassait l'œuf du dîner
avec un couteau sombre
pour après s'endormir
dans l'odeur du ravin
que dominait la fête.

THE WONDER

The bearded girl
was shown off to the curious
and those who went on their way
in the fairground sunset
while she
her day's work done
cracked the supper egg
with a dull knife
in order to sleep well
amid the smell out of the ravine
that overwhelmed the festivities.

ÉGLOGUE

Dans la maison refermée
il fixe un objet dans le soir
et joue à ce jeu d'exister
un fruit tremble
au fond du verger
des débris de modes pompeuses
où pendent les dentelles
des morts
flottent en épouvantail à l'arbre
que le vent fait gémir
mais sur un chêne foudroyé
l'oiseau n'a pas peur de chanter
un vieillard a posé sa main
à l'endroit d'un jeune cœur
voué à l'obéissance.

ECLOGUE

In the house shut up once more
he eyes a single object in the dark
and so plays out this game of how to live
a fruit dangles
at the bottom of the orchard
debris of an old-fashioned glamour
trailing its lace
the dead
swing like scarecrows in a tree
set creaking by the wind
an old man has set his hand
on the heart of a youth
who has vowed to obey it
while a bird sings from a blasted oak
without a trace of fear.

LE BOURG AU SOIR

Des souffreteux geignent au bourg
près de petites lumières
le phosphore au bout d'une allumette
éclate en une cuisine immense
les poiriers aux murs s'incrustent
au milieu des vapeurs nobles.
Personne ne peut dicter
sa lettre à la paysanne
qui se courbe pour l'écrire
dans la plus grande des maisons
et ce soleil qui la frappe
glace en rouge des croisées
douces à qui fait son tour du monde.

TOWN AT EVENING

All over town beside their little lights
the suffering complain
the phosphorus tip of a match
flares up in a huge kitchen
whose walls seem embossed
with pear trees heavy with aromas.
There is no one to dictate the letter
the farm girl wishes to write
bowed over the page
in the largest house of all
and this last light lashing it
glazing the mullions red
a sight sweet to one who's toured the whole earth.

LE RETOUR

Entre une fillette pour réclamer son père
chez le marchand de vin
il sacre mais finalement suit
la silhouette pâle à la natte ouvragée
qui marche de l'avant
tournant parfois la tête
pour s'assurer qu'elle a bien sur ses pas
cet ivrogne las à la blouse glacée
et dont sourit l'épouse
le buste pris dans un corsage d'ombre.

THE RETURN

Come to the wine merchant's house
a little girl seeks to bring her father out
he curses but at last he follows
that pale figure her hair well-plaited
who walks in front
at times turning her head
to see if he's still there
at her heels
this weary drunkard in stiff overalls
whose wife is smiling
her breasts cupped tightly by a blouse of shadow.

PROMENEUR

Qui donc porte manteau à col de velours
et ce chapeau rigide et sombre
alors qu'est venu le moment
que les peaux les plus douces
se lassent de caresses
et vont chercher la paix des ombres ?
Ils peuvent bien tous dormir
l'âne le bœuf et le vieux lièvre
lui veille dans le chemin qui mène
à la maison jaune à solives
et fait tourner entre ses doigts
une fleur cueillie à la haie.

STROLLER

Who then wears the velvet-collared overcoat
and the hat so stiff and dark
now that the moment's come
when the softest flesh
wearies of caresses
and seeks the peace of shadows?
All may well be asleep
the ass and ox and aged hare
but his vigil remains on the path leading
to the house of yellow half-timbers
rolling between his fingers
a flower culled from the hedgerow.

LA CHOUANNE

Dans l'épaisseur du vieux monde
ayant enlevé toute parure
et regardant son corps
dans la lumière
exultait la chouanne
et son cheval gris hennissait
fixé dans l'enclos silencieux
servant l'histoire et la magie
pourvu d'un cœur et de poumons
et tout ce ciel au-dessus d'eux
serait celui des assemblées
et celui des guerres inouïes.

THE CHOUANNE

In the layeredness of the world as it once was
having stripped off all finery
and peering at her body
in the light
the Chouanne exulted
and her gray horse whinnied
secure in the silent paddock
being of sound heart and lungs
in the service of enchantment and history
and over them all the same sky
whether there would be Assemblies
or unspeakable wars.

RIGUEURS ET DÉLICES

Une peinture en trompe-l'œil
fait les délices d'une servante
le vent déchire un ciel de tourment
on abat les cartes
dans le triomphe de la vie
une inconnue approche
qui sait des postures
éblouissantes
et la haie abrite près des nids
toute l'acidité des baies
mais que d'oiseaux
nous restent étrangers
que de couples s'éloignent !

RIGORS AND PLEASURES

A trompe-l'oeil painting
arouses the imagination of a servant girl
the wind tears open an agonized sky
one lays cards down
in the triumph of life
this stranger comes nearer
who knows how to turn her body
dizzyingly
and besides the nests the hedgerow shelters
all the acidity of berries
yet so many birds
remain foreign to us
so many in pairs keeping their distance!

CHIEN AUX ÉCOLIERS

Les écoliers par jeu brisent la glace
dans un sentier
près du chemin de fer
on les a lourdement habillés
d'anciens lainages sombres
et ceinturés de cuirs fourbus
le chien qui les suit
n'a plus d'écuelle où manger tard
il est vieux
car il a leur âge.

THE STUDENTS' DOG

The schoolboys for a lark are smashing up the ice
on the footpath
near the railway
someone has dressed them
in dour wool hand-me-downs
belted with delapidated leather
the dog who follows them
no longer has his own bowl to eat from
for he is old
being their age.

EFFACEMENT

L'herbe a grandi au fossé profond
l'homme en marchant fixe
le nuage étiré
frangé comme son habit gris
des chiens aux horizons béants
diversement aboient
pourtant c'est la paix
le jour va s'incliner
il faudra bien encore
couper le pain à la nuit
assis sur le billot rustique
aven en fin de compte
l'impensable mort.

ERASURE

Grass has grown up in the deep gully
the man out walking stares
at the elongated cloud
fringed like his own gray clothes
dogs in their various ways
bay at the gaping horizons
and yet this is peacetime
the passing day begins to nod
we will again need
to slice our bread at night
seated on rustic benches
when all is said and done
with unfathomable death.

LES ADIEUX

L'homme entend
l'horloge à chiffres noirs
près des plis du rideau mouvant
n'osant poser
le clou qui va rompre le plâtre
regardant courir la moulure
sur la porte qui ferme mal
tout près des adieux s'éternisent
doucereux et las
sous le toit de chaume autrefois clair
mais devenu couleur de bure.

GOODBYES

The man hears
the clock with the black numerals
near the unquiet folds of the drapery
and doesn't dare
drive the nail that will break the plaster
gauging how the molding
runs over the door that closes badly
against the goodbyes going on forever
mawkish and weary
beneath a thatch that was once pale
but is now brown as a cowl.

APPEL CHAMPÊTRE

Un morceau de pain
couvert de raisiné sombre
est le goûter du garçon assis
sur un mur d'éclatante argile
et ses pieds pendants sont chaussés
de brodequins cloutés de fer ;
lorsqu'on l'appelle de loin
il ne répond pas aussitôt
la même voix
clamant alors plus fort son nom
à l'unique syllabe brève
trouble à peine le calme des iles.

CALL OF THE COUNTRY

A wedge of bread
covered with dark grape jam
is the after-school snack
of the boy seated on a wall
of burnished clay
whose dangling feet are shod
in laced boots with metal studs;
when someone calls out from a distance
he doesn't answer right off
the same voice
crying more loudly his name
with its unique short syllable
that barely ripples the calm of these islands.

VOIX

Des enfants se tenaient par la main
mais le plus grand seul parlait
au nom de tous il expliquait
et des écharpes vertes
flottaient sur l'horizon
une femme jardinière
défaisait ses bas sombres
c'était le soir c'était la terre
aux haies épineuses
aux branches mortes
à la fleur.

VOICE

The children held hands
but only the tallest one spoke
in the name of them all he explained
and their green scarves
fluttered on the horizon
a woman gardening
rolled down her dark stockings
this was evening this was earth
for the thorny hedges
for the dead boughs
nearly in flower.

PIERRES ET CORPS

Des pierres de toujours
ou précieuses ou de foudre
des plus aiguës qui tombent
sur le champ du voisin
de celles du bord des mers
les corps vivants s'inquiètent
dans leurs fourrures
et peaux
portant leurs réserves de sang
leurs yeux fragiles
et leurs membres qui cherchent.

STONES AND BODIES

Stones of all ages
whether precious ones or those honed
by lightning hurled
onto the neighbor's field
or those edging the oceans
trouble these living bodies
in their furs
and skins
which are bearing their reserves of blood
their glassy eyes
and questing limbs.

SOUS LES CIEUX

C'était la ferme au beau pressoir
aux cœurs les mieux placés
il en partait des voix chantantes
des lézards y venaient
toute une heure
qui durait comme un siècle d'homme.
Le bruit que fait
la chute d'une pomme
l'enfant l'entendait
en buvant le lait d'une femme
grave et marquée
sur sa peau hâlée
de grains et de lignes
d'une disposition unique
dans l'ordre des créatures.

UNDER THE HEAVENS

This was the farmstead with the fine cider press
for hearts in the right place
voices came from it singing
the advent of lizards there
lasted for what seemed
a human century.
The noise
made by an apple falling
a child heard
while drinking milk from an unsmiling woman
her bronze skin marked
by lines and mottlings
of singular arrangement
in the disposition of creatures.

PRÉSENCE

La villageoise qui n'aime pas sa fille
brandit contre elle
un imaginaire bâton
le cartel bat dans la ténèbre
elle n'a point sommeil encore
cette jeune tête menacée
d'où jusqu'à mi-corps descend
l'ample chevelure
qui croît, fauve, jour et nuit.

PRESENCE

She doesn't care much for her daughter
this village woman who brandishes
an imaginary stick against her
the wall clock strikes in the shadows
yet to find any rest
this girl her head tormented
finds armfuls of tawny hair
falling to her waist
and growing and thickening
by day and night.

L'AFFICHE

L'enfant poussant un cercle de tonneau
qui lui sert de fruste cerceau
court seul avec des cris
mais à celui qui vient d'épeler
sous l'N et l'aigle de l'Empire
l'affiche de conscription
le vieillard seulement dit
dans l'embrasement du soleil
en buvant un poiré mousseux :
« le prochain siècle sera pire »
mais passent les amants qui chantent.

THE NOTICE

The child pushing a wine barrel's metal rim
that serves him as a make-shift hoop
is running
alone with his cries
but to the other one who has just spelled out
under the N and the eagle of Empire
a conscription notice
the old man sipping hard cider
in a blaze of sunshine
only says
"the next century will be worse"
whatever the lovers who pass by are singing.

PAYSAGE HUMAIN

O paysage humain
une femme y entre puis en sort
et sourit vers l'horizon
alors on revoit les arbres
la plaine
et la route dure
la maison avec ses nids
la bête un peu alarmée
qui boit le lait sous la lune
avec un bruit si léger
puis revoilà le corsage
et le corps de la beauté.

HUMAN LANDSCAPE

O human landscape
a woman enters it then departs
smiling in the direction of the horizon
so it is one sees the trees again
the plain
and the hard road in
the house with its nests
the animal slightly alarmed
who drinks milk under the moon
lapping it ever so lightly
then it's there again
her blouse
and the body of loveliness.

LE CHAMP

Fertile et doux un champ respire
au soleil d'après-midi
lieu d'herbes hautes
de plantes naines
il y reste d'un âcre journal
un lambeau sec
un corps de femme y projette
une ombre sur les centaurées
beaucoup de bêtes y sommeillent
ayant des réveils innocents
un soldat, un prêtre, un juge
s'arrêtent à voir son étendue
sur son prix et sa luxuriance
portant des pensers différents
sous un ciel en feu.

THE FIELD

Rich and marly a field breathes out
under the afternoon sun
site of tall grasses
and dwarf plants
a bitter diary lies out there
a dry heap
reflections of a woman's life
a shadow atop the thistledown
while many animals are dozing
stirring softly the way they do
a soldier, a priest, a judge
stop to inspect the vista
entertaining various views
as to its cost and splendor
beneath a sky on fire.

ÉVÉNEMENTS

Il est un temps où l'eau s'agite
puis elle stagne
et la guerre vient
sont exempts de tout murmure
les lichens sur les pierres
mais point la prêle et la ciguë
bercées par un vent tempéré
couper une tige
au fond d'un pré lisse au soir
devient alors
une réussite de la vie
un homme embrassant une fille
survit dans un jardin transfiguré.

WHAT HAPPENS

It is a time of turbulent water
then it stagnates
and war comes
the lichens on stones are exempt
from what's inarticulate
but not so the horsetail and hemlock
rocked by a mild wind
cutting a stem
at the far end of a meadow smoothed out by evening
becomes then
an achievement of life itself
a man with his arms around a girl
surviving in a garden transfigured.

Jean Follain was born in 1903 in a small town in Normandy, and moved to Paris at the age of 21. By the time of his accidental death in 1971 (the result of a motorcar accident in the Place de la Concorde), he had became a highly successful jurist, and was emerging as one of the most respected writers of the age. Yet that earlier world of Canisy, the village he memorialized in his most celebrated of several prose volumes, caused him always to refer to himself as a provincial. In brilliantly short, plainspoken, and quiet poems, he could catch, as if in snapshots, the whole aura of a provincial life now lost. Having explicitly rejected Surrealism ("ce n'était pas moi") as well as the abstruser musings of much modern French poetry, Follain came to be acclaimed in his own lifetime with such awards as the Grand Prix de Poésie de l'Académie Française. Now regarded as one of the germinal poets of the period, he has also become a pervasive influence, "even," as the critic John Taylor puts it, "for poets of vastly different aesthetic persuasions."

Kurt Heinzelman co-founded and for ten years edited the award-winning journal *The Poetry Miscellany*; he is currently Editor-at-Large for the *Bat City Review* as well as Editor-in-Chief of *Texas Studies in Literature and Language* (TSLL). He has been a multiple nominee for the Pushcart Prize; his first two books of poetry were both finalists for Poetry Book of the Year from the Texas Institute of Letters; a third, *The Names They Found There*, was published in the spring of 2011. Both a scholar and translator – he has done translations from Spanish, Italian, German, Turkish, and Latin, as well as French – he also serves on the Board of Directors of the Dylan Thomas Prize in Swansea, Wales.